# MORE THAN *Meets* THE *Eye*

## TRUE STORIES OF SEVEN DOLLS

### LEE L. PIERCE

To Georgia,
With Love, Respect, and Awe!

Lee

7/14/2015

# More Than Meets the Eye:
## True Stories of Seven Dolls

Other books by Lee Pierce

In Time for Tea and Other Childhood Stories
Magic Is Where You Are

# More Than Meets the Eye:

## True Stories of Seven Dolls

Lee Lawrence Pierce

To order additional copies of this book, contact:
Xlibris
1-888-795-4274
www.Xlibris.com
Orders@Xlibris.com

© Lee L. Pierce. All rights reserved. Photography:
Susie Guzman, Chris Knight, and Hiroko Okahashi
Editors: Jill Masters and Angela Brooke
Cover design by Andrew Maxwell

# DEDICATION

In memory of my mother

HELEN LAWRENCE

# ACKNOWLEDGMENTS

Suzy Grossman, for several excellent glossy photos for
More Than Meets the Eye: True Stories of Seven Dolls.
Christopher Knight (photo of author for back cover).
His photograph of the spy doll, Perla Negra, captures the soul of that doll.
Hiroko Okahashi, for her paintings, photos, and her belief in me and this book.
Jill Masters, who is a recognized voice coach and narrator.
No words of mine will ever be enough to thank her for her dedication
and belief in me and my doll book.

Special Thanks to my son Shelby Pierce for his consistent support.

Special Thanks and Gratitude to Joey Barrett, her support has been invaluable.

# FRIENDSHIP

There's a miracle called friendship
That dwells within the heart
And you don't know how it happened
Or where it got its start,
But the happiness it brings you
Always gives a special lift,
Then you realize that friendship
Is God's most special gift!

# ENDORSEMENT
## TRITIA HAMILTON

From a bookstore window, a gypsy doll with compelling eyes caught the attention of a thirteen-year-old girl many years ago. Now, long-term collector Lee Pierce shares her insightful perspective on the multilayered world of dolls.

Aptly titled, More Than Meets the Eye: True Stories of Seven Dolls offers a window into new discovery—a window through which we find aspects of the doll world that we may not have imagined existed. The beautifully costumed dolls, which reflect to us aspects of many cultural traditions, may also be seen as contemporary evolution within the ancient lineage of fetishes—inanimate objects with supposed magical powers or considered to be inhabited by a spirit. Through her skills as a storyteller, combined with her sense of history and extensive knowledge of her subject, author Lee Pierce weaves portraits of seven dolls into a cohesive, unique tapestry. Here, we find doll stories that are told by the owners and from the doll's point of view—with warmth and humor, sensitivity, and compassion. Her own appreciation for the expansive world of dolls and related travels that she has delighted in experiencing and sharing through countless talks and lectures is everywhere apparent in More Than Meets the Eye: True Stories of Seven Dolls.

For everyone, from young readers to knowledgeable doll collectors, More Than Meets the Eye: True Stories of Seven Dolls provides a unique and thoughtful view into the diverse family of humanity as reflected in the world of multicultured dolls. One wonders if that's what the Mexican gypsy doll, Perla, had "in mind" all along.

Lee Pierce is blessed with a romantic and a spiritual sense of awe and vibrant excitement at every discovery she makes.

The original "chance taker" Lee has found through her amazing dolls, history, romance, family ties, and discoveries undreamed of.

Here is Lee Pierce, magical, unadorned, and willing to share preoccupations with her readers who will find her and her book treasures more than worth exploring.

Raimond del Noce Senior

Artist

Philadelphia

More Than Meets the Eye

# CONTENTS

# PROLOGUE

Since the beginning of time, the ancient ones believed the spirits of their ancestors were always around, constantly guiding them and providing protection. They had tremendous influence on their daily lives. Primitive cultures depended on medicine men to "catch the spirits" and transform them into images known as "fetishes." Also called "ancestor images," they were considered sacred. Only the medicine men had the ability to perform rituals and the privilege of touching the sacred objects. Children were never allowed to have contact with these dolls. Instead, they were kept busy with daily life, learning from their parents and elders' customs passed down from their primitive ancestors. When girls became women and boys became men, they were taught the importance of the "ancestor images," the knowledge they held, and how to make them.

As the centuries went by, these ancestor images became less and less important. In time, customs were slowly replaced with modern ideas and new beliefs. The reverence of those first primitive ancestor images can easily be overlooked, but their importance lies in the fact that they reflect the history and customs of these people in a myriad of different ways—sometimes in being made into weird and fascinating-looking shapes of bones, sticks of wood, stones, and many other unusual and often rare objects.

Lee Lawrence began her life as a typical young woman growing up in Locust Valley, Long Island, New York. Her education, however, was not at all typical. She and her brothers were sent in their early years to a Quaker School. A few years later, Lee's mother announced that she would be attending a private school in Cold Spring Harbor, New York. Only nine girls between the ages of eleven and thirteen were accepted into the unusual school. All classes were taught on the top of a garage on the Roosevelt, Long Island, property. Lee tried not to show her embarrassment when she was told the name of the school was Turkey Lane School for Polite Young Ladies. The students were given classes in French conversation, English literature, poetry, and history with only a few "boring classes" in math and science. Often, the girls were invited to perform Shakespearian plays and recite reams of memorized poetry for the benefit of their parents. The performances were always given on the lush green layered and landscaped lawn of the Roosevelt property.

A memorable performance of a Shakespeare play, Lee was cast as the donkey in A Midsummer Night's Dream. Playing the role of the donkey, she was told she had to bray as loudly as she possibly could to convince the audience she really was a donkey—and bray she did! During the performance, a small dog named Snippy, who belonged to the headmistress, suddenly broke away from his owner's arms, bounded up the lawn before anyone could stop him, and took a bite out of the donkey's rear end! Lee got a standing ovation!

After three unforgettable years at Turkey Lane, Lee was sent to a boarding school in Concord, Massachusetts, called Concord Academy. There, she was placed into three different levels. She was far ahead in French, literature, and history. Much to her embarrassment, however, she had had to sit in with the junior classes in math and science.

Three years later, her mother offered her the opportunity to spend a few summer months in Mexico City to learn a new language and a new culture. Lee jumped at the chance. Off she went to Mexico to be the guest of a woman who took in American girls as paying guests. She enjoyed the experience immensely and begged her mother to let her stay a few more months. It was almost an entire year before she returned to America. Her admittance into the University of Mexico as a "listener" changed her life. She would never again follow a conventional education.

By the time she had returned home, she had become fairly fluent in the Spanish language and made the decision to pursue further study of the Spanish language and culture instead of attending a four-year American college. As she wasn't sure which country to visit first, she decided she had better complete the necessary credits for high school before doing any more traveling. She attended a two-year college in New York City graduating with a high school diploma, a certificate for two years of college, and a secretarial degree in shorthand, typing, and business Portuguese.

At the time, the Portuguese business course didn't appear to make any sense at all, but she became good friends with her teacher. To her delight, her teacher invited her to spend a summer with her and her cousins in Santiago, Chile. She then planned to sign up for a course in the Spanish language and Latin American literature, but that never happened!

Just before Lee arrived in Chile, an epidemic broke out. She found the school closed for the summer. She wasn't sure what to do next, but she knew that she had to be involved in some kind of an educational program. Her Chilean family introduced her to the Jesuit headmaster of the Santiago Law School where she was given permission to "sit in" on the Napoleonic law classes.

Lee's Napoleonic law classes came in very handy when she joined the state department two years later. She was sent to Buenos Aires, Argentina, as a secretary. Napoleonic law was still in use in Argentina. Although her secretarial skills were quite adequate, she managed to convince the staff she would be much more useful teaching children English in the library by reading stories with them and helping with the Exchange of Foreign Students program.

A few days before Lee arrived in Buenos Aires, an uprising was in full force. Juan Peron had become president with his wife, Evita Peron, by his side. As soon as he was sworn in, he announced a new law would be put in place. The law promised that all "forgotten descamisados" (shirtless ones) who wished to work would not only be given jobs but would also be protected from ever being fired unless they committed a crime. The new law displaced thousands of educated people who poured into the streets in a frenzy of fury.

Lee felt no particular fear or concern over the fracas; however, her new boss, the American ambassador, immediately called her into his private office to warn her that the situation had become dangerous. He strongly suggested she socialize only with Americans. This made no sense to Lee. She had become good friends with the ambassador's secretary who had not only introduced her to her Argentine family and friends but on several occasions, had whisked her off on weekends outside the city to learn about the lives of country folk called "gauchos" who gaily introduced her to their "asados" (cookouts) and their "bailes" (dances).

She became infatuated with the gauchos and ended up bringing home three gaucho dolls—a woman holding a gourd with a silver straw from which she could drink her tea called mate; her husband with a guitar; and the leader, called Pepe, dressed in colorful garb.

In her travels, dolls began to catch Lee's attention. This surprised her because she had never had any interest in dolls. Nevertheless, she found herself buying unusual dolls with stories to tell. Thus began a love of dolls and an extensive doll collection.

Lee often wondered if the dolls had influenced her to travel extensively to so many countries—or were they like her Polish doll, Kasha, longing to become part of an international doll family? A Mexican gypsy rag doll had caught her attention in a window of a bookstore in New York City. Lee had a feeling the doll held a dark secret. She was determined to find out what it was.

How can one explain the mystery of a doll? Sometimes the stories dolls tell are frightening. Sometimes they are painful. One of the previous doll owners, Maria, not wishing to dwell on the hardships and terror of her own life in a concentration camp, gave her doll to Lee.

The doll had been given to Maria for safekeeping by her Jewish friend who had died in a concentration camp. Maria's promise to keep the doll from harm had been fulfilled, and now she was giving Lee the doll to add to her collection.

Maria said, "If you will keep Kasha for me, I won't ever again have to look back on such terrible suffering."

She gave Lee one last hug and left. Lee never saw Maria again, but this doll, the third in her collection, still remains in a place of honor in the collection of Lee Pierce of over two hundred dolls from forty countries of the world.

Each doll has a story and perhaps even a secret to share!

All who are curious are invited to step inside the pages of this book and visit the fascinating, mystical, and extraordinary world of dolls.

*Lee Lawrence Pierce*
*2014*

# Perla of Mexico:
## A Spy Story

Recently, Andrea asked herself, "When did dolls come into my life?" It took some time to get the answer. Andrea never had any interest in dolls as a young person. She didn't own a doll. She never played with dolls. She grew up playing sports with her brothers and their friends and had become a happy tomboy. Dolls had never been in her vocabulary.

One day, her mother approached her with a determined look on her face.

"Andrea! You've been a tomboy long enough! You're almost thirteen years old, so I've decided to take you on a mother-daughter visit to New York City. We'll take in some exciting events.

"We'll attend concerts, visit some museums, go to an opera, and have delicious lunches in elegant restaurants. And of course, we'll visit Young's Bookstore on Madison Avenue. My old friend, Mrs. Kimball, the owner of the bookstore, will be glad to see us. You remember Mrs. Kimball, don't you? She always shows you where the latest Nancy Drew books are. You can buy two books for your birthday. Mrs. Kimball will be surprised to see how tall you've grown. Does all this sound like fun to you?"

Andrea answered in a barely audible voice, "Sure, Mom! Thanks!"

"You have to understand, Andrea, that none of this will happen until you have a new wardrobe appropriate for a girl of your age. I'll buy you some pretty skirts, tops, shoes, and one pocketbook that will look attractive with whatever you're wearing."

Andrea was horrified at her mother's decision. It would mean she would miss the baseball game. Her brothers had invited her to be their left fielder for the first time. Andrea turned away so that her mother wouldn't see tears clouding her eyes.

Her mother told her they would be staying at her grandmother's apartment.

They arrived in New York City on a chilly February morning. Andrea's grandmother had loaned them her apartment for a week. They stopped by briefly to leave their luggage and then went straight to the famous bookstore on Madison Avenue. The visit was to change Andrea's life forever.

As soon as they arrived at the bookstore, her mother disappeared inside, but Andrea had become fascinated by the display window that was filled with Mexican travel books. Never had she seen such tall, thin books before, and she was intrigued. Propped up against one of the books was the strangest-looking doll she'd ever seen. She wore a bandana over her hair and a rebozo around her shoulders. She had sparkling coal-black eyes surrounded by a sea of white that gave her a terrified look. She was barefooted. Andrea was sure she had a secret and was determined to find out why she looked so scared.

Suddenly, she heard her mother's voice. "Andrea! Come inside, at once! It's too cold out there." With difficulty, she tore herself away from the doll's hypnotic eyes and entered the bookstore. Her mother had gone to the back of the store, but the owner, Mrs. Kimball, came forward to greet Andrea.

"Andrea," she said, "your mother tells me you're going to have a birthday soon. Do you still enjoy reading Nancy Drew books?"

"Yes, but, Mrs. Kimball," Andrea suddenly blurted out, "could you let me hold the doll in the window just for a minute? I promise I'll be very careful with her."

Mrs. Kimball looked surprised. She'd known Andrea for a long time and knew she had never been interested in dolls.

"I'm sorry, dear," said Mrs. Kimball. "The doll doesn't belong to me. She belongs to a famous doll collector. You'd have to get permission from her. She rents the second floor where she sells her dolls."

Mrs. Kimball informed Andrea that the doll collector would be unhappy if she discovered someone was handling any doll before buying it. However, children have a way of being persistent, and the doll was finally taken out of the window and handed to Andrea. She held the doll close to her, whispering, "I know you have a secret. Tell me what it is! I promise I won't tell anyone."

Andrea's attention was broken by the sound of clicking heels approaching. She looked up and saw the face of a very angry woman. Her dark hair was piled on top of her head, and her high-heeled shoes and pasty white face terrified Andrea. To the small child, the woman looked enormous and threatening.

The woman hissed through her clenched teeth. "You're old enough to know better! You can't buy dolls in bookstores!" With that, she tore the doll away from Andrea and went off, her red high heels clicking angrily as she vanished. Andrea watched in dismay as she disappeared around the bookcases, swinging the doll upside down by one leg. The way she treated the doll infuriated Andrea.

At that moment, as terrified as she was of her, Andrea knew the woman was a really bad person and that somehow, it was up to her to rescue the doll.

Two days later, Andrea dared to defy her parents. She had never done that before. She waited until her mother had left her grandmother's apartment, and with no further hesitation, she returned to the bookstore alone. She had been told by her parents that children were not allowed to cross the city streets without an adult, but there was no adult around, so she crossed the busy streets and came close to being hit by a yellow cab. She finally made it to the bookstore. She looked through the window, but the doll was no longer there. She hurried into the store and raced down the aisles to Mrs. Kimball's office without waiting to be announced.

Mrs. Kimball's cheery voice called out, "Come in! I'm on the phone. I'll be with you in a minute."

Her back was turned to Andrea, but there on her desk laid the Mexican gypsy doll, facedown. Andrea could not believe her eyes! She stood frozen with excitement. Mrs. Kimball turned around. She looked surprised to see Andrea, but Andrea didn't waste a minute.

"Mrs. Kimball!" Andrea said. "I came to ask you about the doll. I want to buy her. I have lots of money." Without waiting for an answer, she fished inside her coat pocket and pulled out ten dollars in nickels, dimes, quarters, and pennies. It was her entire year's allowance. Mrs. Kimball was very gracious.

"My dear," Mrs. Kimball said, "you don't need to pay me for this Mexican gypsy doll. The doll owner left the doll to me, but since I have only one son who would not be interested in dolls, you can take her, and please take your money back."

Andrea heaved a sigh of relief. She couldn't believe her good fortune. "Are you sure you don't want to keep the doll?"

Mrs. Kimball handed her the doll, asking, "Is your mother waiting for you?"

Andrea did not wait to answer. She didn't want her to know she had disobeyed her mother and had come alone to the store. Snatching up the precious doll, she tucked her inside her coat, leaving the year's allowance all over Mrs. Kimball's desk.

"Thank you for the doll, Mrs. Kimball!" Andrea ran out of the store as though it had caught on fire!

Once Andrea and her mother had returned home to Long Island, she hid the doll under her pillow and prayed that her parents wouldn't discover how disobedient she had been. She certainly would also have to keep the doll hidden from her brothers if she didn't want to be teased for the rest of her life for buying a doll at her age!

Days passed. Andrea was so happy with the amazing doll with the terrified-looking eyes. She told her over and over again, "You don't need to be scared anymore. You'll be safe with me. Mrs. Kimball told me you're a Mexican gypsy. I think I'll name you Perla Negra—Black Pearl. But I'll just call you Perla. Would that be all right with you?" Hearing no resistance from her doll, Andrea officially gave her the name Perla Negra.

There was a knock on the door. Andrea ran to open it, thinking it was her friend Anna. Instead, a large man wearing a trench coat with the collar turned up high on his neck and a hat pulled down over his eyes stood in the doorway.

"Are you Ms. Lawrence?" said the man in a deep, demanding voice.

"Yes! But I'm not allowed to talk to strangers," she said, trying with all her might to close the door, but the man wedged his foot in the way.

"Please get your mother, young lady," he said. Instead, Andrea ran into her room and shut the door. She was trembling. Instinctively, she knew something terrible was about to happen. She grabbed Perla and hid her under her pillow, wanting to make sure she was safely hidden. A few minutes later, her mother came into the room and demanded she turn over the doll immediately.

"Do you know what FBI stands for, Andrea?" She sounded furious. Andrea looked down and shook her head. "FBI stands for Federal Bureau of Investigation. The FBI officer tells me you bought a doll at Young's Bookstore, and they want it. And by the way, Andrea, how much did you pay for that doll?"

Hanging her head, she answered her mother in a whisper, "Ten dollars."

"That means you spent your entire year's allowance on a doll? Give me that doll at once!" Andrea burst into tears.

"Give her to me this minute!" she said. "I will tell your father, and you will learn what punishment you'll receive for being disobedient and stupid.

Andrea pulled the precious doll out from under her pillow. "Oh, Perla! I'm so sorry," she whispered.

Her mother was standing right by the bed. "Now!" was all she said.

Andrea handed her the doll.

"Will they give me back my doll, Mother?" she asked, choking down a sob.

"I don't know," said her mother, slamming the door and marching off with Perla.

Andrea couldn't remember ever feeling a moment more painful. Never before had she seen her mother so angry.

Soon, Andrea discovered she had lost all interest in playing sports with her brothers. All she could think of was Perla. Where was she? How long would it take the FBI before returning her doll? She sat down in total misery, and with tears streaming from her eyes, she wrote a poem:

Perla, oh my Perla!

Why did they take you away?

You don't belong to anyone but me,

So, wherever you are

I know you hear me speaking.

You're an amazing doll,

With flashing black hypnotic eyes

Listen to me. Hear me, Perla!

I've risked a lot to save you.

I've even told lies, so no matter what,

Get back to me as soon as possible.

We belong together, you and I.

I'm not sure why,

But I'd better quit writing.

I'm going to cry—cry hard,

Because, Perla, I love you.

I love you so much.

They had no right to take you away.

You don't belong to anyone but me.

Several weeks later, a package arrived addressed to Andrea. She ran into her room, shut the door, and with trembling hands, unwrapped the package. There she was! Her mystery doll, Perla Negra! She was so happy to have her back that, at first, she didn't notice her neck. Something didn't feel right. Looking closely, she suddenly realized that Perla's head must have been removed and then sewed back on. But why? She was horrified. The doll had become so real to her. Andrea began to whisper to her as though she was a real person.

"Perla! Did you always have a scarred neck?" Andrea was sure she heard her whispering "no!"

It was some years later that Andrea found the answer to her question. Unknown to her at the time, the FBI had gone on the theory that an American spy was sending messages to the Japanese in the heads of dolls. After removing several of the dolls' heads, they decided that was not the case. In the meantime, Andrea kept questioning Perla.

"Tell me who hurt you, Perla. Please tell me. I promise I won't tell anyone else." But Perla's frightened eyes only convinced Andrea she had a reason to be scared.

Several weeks had gone by since the FBI had returned Perla. The boys had stopped teasing Andrea when they heard the doll had belonged to a spy. They went back to playing their Sunday games, and Andrea began dreaming of traveling to learn about other people in places far away.

When Andrea turned sixteen, her mother asked her if she'd like to spend a summer studying in Mexico City. Andrea jumped at the idea. The trip to Mexico was arranged. She would be taking a train all the way to Mexico City. Her mother would accompany her as far as Saint Louis, but for the rest of the trip, she'd be traveling alone. She was told that her hostess, Señora Martinez del Rio, with whom she'd be staying, would meet her on arrival. Never before had Andrea felt more terrified, but she didn't admit her fear as the trip would be canceled.

Her summer stay turned into ten of the most memorable months Andrea had ever spent anywhere. The greatest thing to come from all those months in Mexico was to discover that her Spanish was now close to perfect.

In 1950, Andrea was living in New York City. She opened her bedroom window wide one morning to breathe in some fresh April air. Looking down below in the street, she noticed that a great deal of commotion was taking place. Then she heard a newspaper boy yelling, "Read all about it! The mystery of the 'Doll Lady' has been solved! Read all about it!"

Andrea closed the window, threw on her coat, and dashed into the hallway to get the elevator. Almost all the papers had been sold, but she managed to get one of the last copies. Back in the apartment, she read all about the "Doll Lady," a Mrs. Dickinson, who had just been released from jail. As she studied the photo on the page, she was convinced that this was the very same terrifying woman in the bookstore who had grabbed Perla out of her hands. Could that be true? She kept on reading, hoping to learn everything about this woman. She wanted to know more about Perla as well. The article told her nothing about how Mrs. Dickinson had acquired the doll Andrea now possessed or where she had bought her. She spent the next several months researching the story to find out that Perla had been found in a flea market in Mexico.

"You know," mused Andrea one day, "I do believe that if Perla could talk, I'd be able to understand her now that I have lived in Mexico. Dear Perla, can you speak? If you are able to, will you please tell your story in your own words?" To Andrea's amazement, Perla began to speak.

## THE MEXICAN GYPSY DOLL SPEAKS

"Si, querida!" Querida means "dear one" in Spanish. "I will tell you the story. I come from a large family. We are gypsies. I had many brothers and sisters. We were very poor. One day, my mother came to me with tears in her eyes and told me I could bring in lots of money because 'your eyes are made of genuine black pearls.' She took me to the mercado in the city. The vendor bought me for very little money, although it seemed a fortune to us. He took me and placed me on a high shelf. He didn't think anyone would buy me because of my strange-looking eyes. Then one day, several weeks later, an American couple stopped by. The man asked the vendor how much the Mexican gypsy doll would cost."

"'For you, señor, very little! Only fifteen pesos! It's a bargain. The doll's eyes are made of genuine Mexican pearls.'"

"The man's wife began to protest vehemently.

"'Are you crazy? Those eyes are glass eyes. They most certainly are not pearls! How can you fall for such a lie?' But the husband persisted.

"'There is something special about this doll. I will buy her. I believe she will someday teach you about love.'

"'Don't be ridiculous! If you buy that doll, keep it out of my sight. She's the ugliest doll I've ever seen. I won't have her in my doll collection.'

"I was handed to Mr. Dickinson by the vendor. He held me gently in his hands for a long time. Then he turned to his wife and said, 'You don't have to believe what I am saying right now, but someday you will see that what I am telling you will come true. I will buy this doll for your doll shop.'

"I was so happy someone liked me enough to buy me. Besides, gypsies love going to different places. I heard in their conversation that we'd be going to New York City in America.

"I was wrapped up in a newspaper and handed back to the man with the angry wife. When we arrived in the big city called New York, I was more excited than I'd ever been.

"One day in Mrs. Dickinson's doll shop, a man entered the second floor. Mrs. Dickinson greeted him enthusiastically. He was from Japan. They talked for a long time. Then the man said he had to go but to be sure to let him know when it was safe to come back. At that moment, with a gypsy's sharp intuition, I realized that something unspeakable was about to take place. I just didn't know what it was.

"Mrs. Dickinson went on to say that she would have the bookstore owner put me in a window display. She warned the Japanese man not to come inside the store if I was not in the window.

"'It would be too dangerous,' said Mrs. Dickinson. I wondered why. "I was placed in the window. What fun! I could now watch all the people passing by. My eyes seemed to attract a lot of attention.

"A few days passed. Suddenly, I saw a young girl with her nose pressed against the store window. She was looking at me and seemed fascinated. The sun was brilliant. My eyes sparkled.

"Shortly thereafter, I was lifted from the window and handed to the child. I hoped she would buy me and take me home with her."

After working for several years at a couple of small jobs, Andrea was finally offered a job with an organization called Radio Free Europe. She was now living with her parents in New York City and had settled into a brand-new life with her gypsy doll, the centerpiece of her bedroom. She was beginning to collect other dolls. The very first doll she had acquired had been a gift from her grandfather who had presented her with a beautiful Japanese dancing doll in a tall glass case. Perla was the only doll Andrea needed, or so she thought. Yet as much as she loved Perla, Andrea's love never seemed to change the look of terror in the doll's eyes. She promised Perla that as soon as she had made enough money, she would take her to see the famous doll restorer to get her eyes fixed. She felt that her beloved doll didn't want to terrify people anymore.

As soon as Andrea had been given her first paycheck, she went to Madison Avenue to introduce Perla to a well-known doll restorer. She knew it was going to cost a lot of money to have the white taken from the doll's eyes, but she wanted to get rid of her scary glare.

"How much will you charge?" she asked the restorer. At first, he didn't seem to hear her. He was looking intently at Perla's eyes. Finally, he looked up at Andrea.

"Miss, do you realize the eyes of this doll are made of genuine black Mexican pearls?"

"Oh no, sir!" Andrea begged to differ. "The doll belonged to Mrs. Dickinson. She was considered to be the most famous doll collector in the world. She scoffed when her husband told her the eyes were real pearls and told him 'those eyes are glass. They are definitely not pearl eyes.'"

The restorer finally convinced Andrea that he knew what he was talking about and told her it would cost five hundred dollars to restore the eyes. "You have to understand this is a very delicate job," said the doll restorer. "I must be careful not to scratch the eyes. Do you wish to leave her with me? It will take at least a week to complete the job."

Andrea gasped. She couldn't bear to be without Perla for an entire week but decided there was no choice. She would have to wait until she had received three checks from her work. Once Perla was admitted, Andrea called the doll hospital constantly to make sure everything was all right. Finally, she had the money in hand; and on her lunch hour, she ran to pick up Perla. The transformation was incredible. Perla was now a beautiful doll with a sweet, mysterious smile. Andrea was convinced she had made the right decision.

One evening, she was sitting in her bedroom. She went over to the bookshelf where Perla and the Japanese dancing doll had been placed. They looked beautiful there. She had painted her bookshelf a vibrant blue and had placed a soft light over it. The dolls looked a little lonely. Andrea thought she heard Perla whispering, "I'm missing my friends and family. Can you find me some more friends?"

"Sure, Perla, I'll look," Andrea assured her. "Shall I buy another doll from your country?"

The answer came back. "That would be nice, but I want to meet dolls from all over the world."

Through the years, Andrea collected two more Mexican dolls then added three Argentinean dolls and two priceless dolls from China. Andrea's mother had also bought her a Spanish dancing doll with a silly expression on its face. With a twinkle in her eye, she claimed the expression reminded her of Andrea when she performed a paso doble. Andrea was not particularly amused, but the doll was cute. She named her Silly Lita.

# Kasha of Poland:
## Escape from a Death Camp

After three weeks of being at her new job with Radio Free Europe, Andrea became discouraged. The desk next to her was still empty. She had decided a friend would be nice to have. The desk remained vacant until finally, one afternoon, her boss appeared and introduced her to a young woman from Czechoslovakia. He told Andrea her full name, but try as she might, Andrea never could pronounce or remember the young lady's last name. She remained forever Maria to her. Andrea soon discovered that Maria spoke many languages, including Czech, Polish, Russian, Italian, French, and English. She never seemed to have time to leave her desk. Several times, Andrea invited her to be her guest at lunch, but she refused all invitations with a sad, sweet smile, saying, "No, thank you. Maybe next week."

After several months had passed, Andrea couldn't stop wondering who Maria was and why she looked so sad. One afternoon, Andrea suddenly heard herself blurting out. "Maria, I know this sounds silly, but I'd like to invite you to have dinner at my house. I've started a doll collection. I'd love to show it to you. Would you come and dine with me?"

To Andrea's amazement, Maria's face lit up. She said, "I'd love to have dinner with you and see your doll collection. May I ask a favor of you?"

"Ask me anything, Maria," Andrea said.

"May I bring a doll I've had for a long time and tell you the doll's personal story?"

They agreed to meet the following Saturday. Maria arrived that evening carrying a small bag. Andrea welcomed her, taking her straight to her bedroom where she showed her the blue bookcase and the dolls.

"Thank you so much for coming, Maria. I know how busy you are."

"It's not that I'm busy, Andrea. It's that I've been trying to make a very difficult decision as to how I am to live the rest of my life. It's taken all this time to realize that you are the one that can help me do this."

Andrea was amazed.

"How can I do that, Maria? I'll be happy to do anything I can to help, but . . ."

"All I'm asking," said Maria, "is for you to listen to my story. I have brought you this doll so that—" Before she could finish her sentence, Andrea interrupted.

"But, Maria, you need not give me any presents."

"This is not a gift from me, Andrea. It's a gift that only you can give to me. I'll try to explain."

Andrea nodded. She was longing to meet this new doll.

Maria reached into the bag. Unwrapping the slightly damp newspaper, she removed the bubble wrap that was protecting the doll. Sounding apologetic, she said, "I'm afraid Kasha is quite damaged."

Andrea saw right away what she meant. The doll's white-blonde hair worn in two pigtails was disheveled and messy. Her right hand had lost a finger, and her left side had no hand at all. Her brightly colored skirt was wrinkled and torn. Her red boots were badly scuffed. Most amazing of all was the deep sadness Andrea saw in the doll's eyes. Her eyes reminded her of the look of sadness in Maria's eyes.

"This doll has lost the garland of colorful flowers that once was worn on her blonde hair," said Maria.

Intuitively, Andrea sensed that this doll had a great deal to do with Maria's life. It was probably the reason for her not wanting to socialize on the job. In the stillness of her bedroom, Andrea reached for Maria's hand.

"Please tell your story, Maria. I promise I won't interrupt." Maria took a deep breath.

"This doll, Kasha, belonged to my best friend, Hiya Rose," she began. "We met on a cruise when we were eight years old and spent most of the time playing together with Kasha. When it came time to say good-bye, we both cried. Our parents realized that a deep friendship had taken place. They consoled us by making us a promise.

"'We'll all get together every summer for a week at the same time. Sometimes we'll meet in Krakow, Poland. Then, Hiya Rose, we can visit Maria in Czechoslovakia,' said Hiya Rose's father.

"Our friendship grew stronger with each passing year. We became like sisters. When I was almost sixteen, it was decided that I was old enough to make the trip on my own to Krakow, Poland. I was thrilled by my parent's decision, and off I went to Krakow. I couldn't wait to see my old friend and tell her about some new stories I had written for Kasha. I felt happy to be back in Poland, but there was an unexplained feeling about this marvelous, old city. There seemed to be many less people around laughing and chatting in the streets. I wondered why. When I was pulled through the familiar door of Hiya Rose's house and embraced by the entire family, I forgot about my misgivings and didn't bother to ask what might be going on, but Hiya Rose, feeling something was not right, worried about her parents. She felt they must have been hiding some dark secret from her. She finally asked them, 'Mama, Papa, why are you both looking so nervous and distraught?'

"'Hiya Rose,' said her father, 'there are cruel people in the world. We believe they will soon be in Krakow.'

"Two days later, just as the family was finishing dinner, there was a loud knock on the door. I saw the family looking frozen. Germany had invaded Poland, and it wasn't long before citizens were being rounded up and taken away. The loud knock had turned into a kicking sound as though someone was trying to break the door down with a heavy boot.

"'Quick, girls! Go into your bedroom and hide under the bed,' said Hiya Rose's mother.

"We fled into the bedroom and slid quickly under the bed. Hiya Rose grabbed Kasha off her rocking chair.

"'Listen, Maria!' she whispered. 'These must be the bad men my family told me about. If they catch us, they will kill us.'

"We huddled together under the bed, barely breathing.

"'You must promise that if anything happens to me, you will never let anything happen to Kasha. Will you promise?' she pleaded.

"'I promise, Hiya Rose.' I was too terrified to say anything else. Hiya Rose passed Kasha to me, saying in a barely audible voice, 'Quick! Hide in the closet under the clothes. They won't find you there!' We hugged each other tearfully. I slipped into the dark closet, hiding Kasha under my skirt and burying us both under a pile of clothes.

"The front door gave way with a crashing sound. Two German officers in Nazi uniforms marched through the small house, yelling and demanding our attention. 'Come along, you swine!' they said.

"We could hear Hiya Rose's father pleading, 'Do not resist, wife! They will harm us more.' There was no further sound from either parents, but you could hear the officers dragging them across the room. The door slammed. The minutes passed interminably. It didn't take them long to reappear. They came into the bedroom and found Hiya Rose under the bed. They grabbed her. She didn't utter a sound.

"I heard them leaving. Then a deafening silence followed. I shifted a little in the closet. One of the Nazi officers returned to the bedroom and began shouting, 'We have no time for games! If you're in the closet, come out, or we'll start shooting.' Slowly I emerged. I was pulled roughly by the arm out into the cold, rainy night and tossed into a huge van, landing on a child huddled in the arms of his mother. The child began to cry. The mother covered her child's mouth with her hand.

"Muffled sobs finally died out. The vehicle was crammed with people of all ages, including young children who were so terrified that all they could do was stare at me with wide eyes. The frozen fear permeated the atmosphere of the old truck. With a rough jerk, the truck started rattling down the road. No one had any idea where we were going.

"Hours later, the truck came to a stop. It was pouring rain. No one had eaten. Most of the old people were suffering terribly from the long, cold ride. They hauled everyone out, shouting, 'Schnell! Schnell!' and kicking at anyone who staggered too close to their muddy boots. Unknown to us, the bedraggled prisoners, we had arrived outside the gates of one of the most infamous death camps in Poland called Treblinka. Without a second thought, I fell to the ground and quickly pulled Kasha from under my clothes and started to bury her.

"'Hey, you! What do you think you're doing? Steh'auf! Get up, now!'

"There was chaos all around as people were being shoved and prodded by the German guards. The guard caught sight of me on the ground. He hauled me up roughly and tossed me

through the tall, foreboding gates but not before I had a chance to cover over the spot where Kasha now lay buried in the mud."

Maria hesitated in the telling of her story. Andrea wasn't sure Maria was going to be able to continue.

"Then what happened?" Andrea asked in a whisper.

"I thought every day would be my last day on earth," Maria said.

She spoke of her parents. She explained how grateful she was that they had decided to stay home on that fateful day. At least they were safe and probably praying that she had somehow been able to escape.

"The screams of the people were too horrible to describe, as one by one, they were stripped and ordered into what I now know were the dreaded gas chambers. And yet, it was so strange that many of them walked naked, without uttering a sound to their burning deaths.

"As the days went on," said Maria, "I began to think of the buried Kasha as a real living child. I knew I had to rescue her. I promised Hiya Rose that I would always keep her safe.

"It was a cruel winter that year, with endless rain and sleet most every day as I remember.

"Maybe it was heaven weeping for us all. All I wanted to do was to get to Kasha and unbury her from her muddy grave. I didn't even know what I would actually do after that, but I envisioned over and over again running away from that living hell.

"One freezing night, I waited until the huge gates swung open to let in the changing of the guards. I managed to slip through and was just about to dig up Kasha. Out of the dark, a brilliant spotlight blinded me. I was dragged back inside by my hair and beaten. I was threatened and told to never try such an escape again if I wished to live, but once again, the thought of Kasha being buried in the cold was more than I could bear. I tried again and was caught a second time and beaten even more severely. 'The next time you try to escape, fraulein, I'll shoot you in the head,' the German guard said in a quiet, controlled voice. His remark cut through me like a sharp knife."

Maria and Andrea sat in silence. Then Maria, hugging Kasha close to her, said in a soft voice, "Let Kasha tell her story, now."

## KASHA SPEAKS

"Hello! I'm a Polish doll. Before I was damaged, I lived in a doll shop. I'd been sitting around on the shelf for a long time. I longed for someone to buy me. One day, a woman came in. She stood by the shelf where I'd been placed. She picked me up and asked the shop owner, 'How much is this doll? I'd like to buy her.'

"If I'd been human, I would have jumped for joy. I was then wrapped and taken to the woman's home. Once there, I was carefully rewrapped in beautiful, colorful paper.

"The next day was her daughter's seventh birthday. Suddenly, a little girl came skipping into the living room. Wrapped in my festive paper and unable to see anything, I could only imagine what it felt like to be human. I think what humans call seeing one another for the first time and loving one another right away—'love at first sight.'

"'Good morning, Mama! Today is my birthday!' said the small girl.

"'I know, my dear! I have a present for you.'

"Her mother handed me, in all my beautifully wrapped paper and fancy bows, to her daughter. As she watched her daughter opening the gift, she smiled.

"The child's name was Hiya Rose. With trembling hands, she carefully opened the package. When she saw me, she let out a shriek of delight.

"'Oh, Mama! What a beautiful doll! I will love her forever. Thank you. Thank you so much.'

"She threw her arms around her mother's neck and ran back into her bedroom. Sitting down on her bed and holding me close to her, she said, 'Let's see! What shall I call you? I know! I will name you Kasha. Do you like that name?'

"I, Kasha, wanted to tell her, 'I love that name!' I was so happy to have a name at long last.

"A year went by. Hiya Rose's parents decided to take her on a week-long cruise for her eighth birthday. She was a pale, delicate child, but oftentimes, I would overhear her father telling her that she had the courage of many lions.

"'Oh! Can I take Kasha with me? Please, please!'

"When she was told she could indeed take me with her, she danced around the room swinging me by my arms. We were happy. I had never traveled on deep waters. I was as excited as Hiya Rose was to go on this journey.

"On the big ship, Hiya Rose met another girl her own age. She was named Maria and had pink cheeks and wonderful hazel eyes with specks of green that became visible in the sunlight. By the end of the trip, the two little girls had become such good friends while playing with me that they both cried when they had to say good-bye.

Our parents realized a deep friendship had taken place. They consoled us by making us a promise that we would meet each summer either in Poland or Czechoslavia.

"With each summer visit, the friendship became stronger and stronger. The girls dressed me up and had tea parties for me. They read to me. They even took the time to make me a doll house with a kitchen, a living room, a bathroom, and a pretty pink bedroom. They made all sorts of delicious food with pastries that they always ate at the end of their playtime. They pretended to feed me all the delicacies before they finished them off.

"Those were the very best days of my entire life. I never imagined what would happen next. All I remember is Hiya Rose and myself hiding under the bed. Then Hiya Rose handed me to Maria, telling her to hide in the closet. But Hiya Rose was discovered in no time. Then I was found, dragged from the closet, and tossed into a truck. I was hidden in Maria's clothes until she buried me deep in the mud just outside the tall barbed fence of the dreadful death camp called Treblinka. At that moment, I was glad I was a doll and couldn't feel the cold. Then came a long, dark silence."

Andrea looked at Maria as the silence settled over the bedroom. "Then what happened?" Andrea asked in a whisper.

"I could think of nothing else but saving Kasha," Maria said. "She had become my child. I had to rescue her.

"Late one evening, a violent storm raged outside. All the lights, especially the hateful search lights, went out. Then a thick fog engulfed the entire camp. Crouching down low, I almost managed to get to the gate without being intercepted. Then I stopped, realizing I was dangerously close to someone. It was a guard standing on duty close to the gate. The pouring rain and thick fog had become my best friends. The ghostly figure turned in my direction. I lay in the mud and rain, scarcely daring to breathe. A car's horn pierced the thick black night air. A car door slammed. A voice rang out, 'Damn! What a bloody night! Open the gate, Gustav, before we both drown!' The gate flew open. A second figure appeared—that of a huge man. He walked rapidly through the gate.

"'It's about time you got here, Heinrick! What took you so long? Hurry! We've saved dinner and some very fine wine for you.' The two men hastily embraced. I quickly slipped through the tall gates, and not one minute too soon, the gates slammed shut. I crawled through the rain and mud. I found the place, clearly remembering where I had buried Kasha. I began digging frantically. At last, I felt the doll beneath my hands and pulled her out of her muddy grave. I held her, whispering, 'I am here, little Kasha. I have some new stories and messages from Hiya Rose, but we have to hurry, so I won't speak anymore.'

"There was no more fear left to be had. I just knew I'd escaped and had to keep going to fulfill my promises to Hiya Rose. I crawled the whole night through until daybreak. I passed out somewhere. I don't remember where. But by the grace of God, I wasn't picked up by the gestapo. I have no memory as to who found me. It took me weeks to recuperate."

As Andrea listened to Maria's story, tears filled her eyes. Maria turned to her, and once again, she reached for Andrea's hand. Then with a slight sob, she whispered, "Kasha saved my life."

Andrea asked, "How did you ever get to New York City?"

"It's a long, complicated story," Maria said. "Let's just say that angels brought me here, and always, I had my Kasha with me." She looked at Andrea with her sad eyes and asked, "Andrea, will you keep Kasha for me?"

Andrea threw her arms around Maria and hugged her.

"Of course, I'll keep Kasha for you. She'll always have a place of honor in my collection."

Maria returned Andrea's hug, saying, "Because you have taken Kasha into your doll family, I have fulfilled my promise to Hiya Rose. Now I can start life anew, putting all the horrors of the Holocaust behind me." She looked at her watch and said, "Andrea, it's late. I must leave now."

With one last grateful hug, Maria left without saying another word.

The next day, Andrea returned to her job. Maria did not appear that day or any other day.

She simply vanished without a trace.

# Silly Lita of Spain:

## A Mother's Gift

A gypsy girl named Lita lived across the seas in Spain. Andrea had once read about her in a doll collector's book filled with photos and stories of dolls from around the world. As she read the story of Lita, Andrea felt as though Lita was speaking to her from the pages of the book. Andrea was mesmerized. She stared at the photos of the real girl who once had a doll made to her exact image by a Spanish doll maker.

### THE GYPSY GIRL LITA SPEAKS

"Hola! My name is Lita Ramirez. I am a Spanish 'gitana,' a gypsy with a story to tell! You may not believe what I'm going to tell you, but when gitanos speak, it is wise to listen. Gitanos know things that most people don't know. We learn from our extensive travels, moving from one place to another, not because we want to but because no one wants us around, so we keep going.

"You may say, 'Don't be silly! Gitanos don't usually take the time to tell their stories.' Or you might ask, 'Why?'

"I'll tell you why. Because no one wants to listen! Besides, gypsies are far too busy traveling from one place to another. If you pay them, they will tell your fortune. Otherwise, to bother to tell their stories to people who scoff at their 'superstitions' is unnecessary. Gitanos can be good friends, but if you are rude or insult them, they can become enemies.

"Also, when gypsies do decide to stay in one place for a while, they keep to themselves. They are very busy making beautiful things such as tablecloths and scarves, lovely straw baskets, jewelry, and many other crafts, all of which can be bought for very little money. They must work hard to survive. Making the most money is when they dance. Gitanos dance with passion.

"I was abandoned when I was a baby. My mother was too poor to feed me. My father left us. He joined another band of gypsies and went off. A young gypsy girl by the name of Alura Flores saw me lying in a blanket by the side of the road. She picked me up, crooning, 'Poor darling! I will take you with me and teach you the art of flamenco dancing and other arts and crafts. I will teach you the history and culture of our background.'

"I loved Alura. She was like the mother I never had. She taught me everything. She taught me the rules of etiquette for gypsies. She taught me to be proud of our inheritance. She explained why we were a proud people. She said that we had descended from royal cultures.

She explained that originally, we had come from Egypt, but traveling through India, Armenia, Iran, and even Greece, our language became a mixture of Punjabi, Hindi, and other Dardic languages. Alura also explained that the gitanos are a nomadic people and speak a language called 'Romani Chib.' I traveled for many years going from one place to another with Alura and her colorful gypsy tribe.

"One day, Alura said, 'Now, Lita! You are almost grown up, so I will teach you the great art of flamenco dancing. Our dancing usually brings in quite a bit of money.'

"She began teaching me how to hold a small thing worn on the fingers of both hands. They were called castanets. Castanets are not easy to play. One castanet has a deeper tone. It represents the 'man.' It's worn on the left hand. The other castanet is the 'woman' worn on the right hand. The woman speaks incessantly. Whatever she says, the man responds, 'Yes, dear! Yes, dear! Yes, dear!'

"When I asked, 'But, Alura, why do gypsies steal? Why are people afraid of us?' She answered, 'People fear us, little Lita, because they've never taken the time to study who we are, where we originally came from, and why we're still forced to do mean things like picking pockets and stealing in order to survive. When gypsies feel they are close to starvation and find themselves fearing they might die in the coldest of climates, they turn to smuggling. They use the beautiful, provocative gypsy women to distract the police. They are often successful and feel no remorse. We are hardworking people but have always been made to live a distance outside of important cities. It's a cruel fate.'

"One day, a year later, I had finally been accepted to dance with the group taught by my adoptive mother. She was also my beloved teacher. I was only fifteen years old. I don't ever remember being so excited. To be invited to dance in the popular square in Barcelona called 'Las Ramblas' was a great opportunity and an honor. Of course, I was very nervous.

"In the audience was a man. I was aware he was watching me with great attention. When the show ended, he told me he was a doll maker and asked me to stop by his gift shop in two weeks. I wondered why and told Alura about the invitation. She agreed to visit the shop. What a surprise when we saw a doll in the window of the shop that looked just like me! She even had that worried look on her face that Alura reminded me I always wore when I danced. I looked again. I couldn't believe it. The doll was me, with that silly-looking expression on my face.

"Then an even more amazing thing happened. A woman came into the store and without hesitating, said, 'That doll is so cute. I'd like to buy her for my daughter. She looks just like that doll when she's dancing a paso doble. How much do you wish for her? And what's her name?'

"'Her name is Lita.'

"The store owner told the American woman how he had recently seen a young gypsy girl dancing and was determined to capture her intense look.

"He suddenly stopped, and walking over to us, he put his hand on my shoulder. He asked the American woman, 'Does she look familiar?'

"'Oh my goodness,' said the American woman as she looked at the doll and then back at me. 'They do look alike! My daughter would be enchanted with this doll. I'll buy her.'

"The doll maker told her, 'I don't really want to sell her, but since you mentioned your daughter has the same funny expression on her face when she dances, I will sell her as a gift to your daughter. What's your daughter's name?'

"'Her name is Andrea,' answered the American woman.

"With that, the doll was wrapped and handed to the woman.

"As Alura and I left the store, she turned to me, saying, 'I'm sorry we didn't get here sooner. I would have bought the doll for you.'"

## LITA THE DOLL SPEAKS

"We all tell Andrea about our joys and our woes because she is the best listener in the world. She loves gypsies. She has studied our culture. What she seems to love the most about us is that there is an element of extreme danger in many of our escapades. 'I flirt with danger,' she once told me, which made me laugh. I know exactly what she is talking about! I almost disappeared with a wild band of gypsies from another section of Spain. They were from a different tribe of gypsies than the one Alura belonged to. I can tell you the story. It was quite disastrous at first, but then again, everything is exciting when gypsies are involved!

"Right after the kind old doll maker had finished making me, he placed me gently on a low shelf in his store. 'They will see you better here ,' he told me later. I was at eye level with anyone who entered the store, and thus, I was in a perfect spot to be seen. I was feeling quite important and especially beautiful with my castanets poised for action when in walked a band of colorful gypsies, all swaying to the rhythm of a fine guitar. Baubles of gold earrings glittered on the exquisite lady gypsies' ears in the fading sunlight of the day. I was thrilled to see them.

"Gypsies had always been good to me. I was admiring one gypsy's bright red skirt when all of a sudden, she hoisted the folds of her full skirt up, and three small children darted out from under it. A young child grabbed me by my middle and ran out of the store. The other gypsies wandered around the store for a moment but not before the doll maker noticed that I was gone and rushed out of the shop shouting at the top of his lungs, 'Stop, thief! Stop this minute!'

"Just as he rounded the corner of the street, the child, still clutching me by my middle, tripped and came crashing to the sidewalk. I was sure I felt a terrible pain in my face and tasted a strange sensation of sand in my mouth. Then everything faded, and I don't remember much of what happened. The next thing I knew, I was back inside the shop with the doll maker. When I looked around the room, no trace of gypsies could I see anywhere. They had all disappeared. The doll maker was gently stroking my wounded face.

"'I will restore your beauty once again, dear, dear Lita. I will fix your face so that no one will ever know that you were dropped and broken by thieving hands,' said the doll maker.

"I thought I saw a tear fall from his sad eyes. But I was never sure if it was a tear or just a bit of sunlight reflected on his cheek. I went to sleep after that and dreamed of dancing in the square while crowds surrounded the band of gypsies that Alura danced with. I was in heaven, twirling in my full-fluted skirt with castanets, talking with the sound of wild guitars. No life is fuller and happier than the life of a dancing gypsy!

"Let me explain as I am a doll—I feel no concern about leaving Spain and becoming a part of an American family, so here I am in Andrea's ever-expanding doll collection. I've been placed here with the other dolls, so this is now my true home. I love being a part of Andrea's collection because I've met so many other dolls from other parts of the world. We also know Andrea loves us, so we take joy in telling her our personal stories. We tell Andrea about our joys and our hardships. We tell her anything she wants to know because we trust her. We know she trusts us. Another thing we know about her is her fascination with gypsies.

"I turned to Andrea, asking, 'Andrea, have you ever met a gypsy that frightened you?'

"'I certainly have, and I never forgot the experience,' said Andrea. 'I was really frightened.'

"'Do tell me the story,' I said.

"'Well,' said Andrea, 'one summer, I was in Barcelona with a group of friends. After spending time sightseeing, we all decided it was time to take a break and sat down at a small café. When I finished my beverage, I told my friends I was going off to find some earrings for a friend. My friends were nervous about me going off alone and tried to stop me, but I assured them there was no need to worry and that I'd be back soon. With that, I left. I was enchanted by the look of a winding street and began walking down it.'

"All of a sudden, I had the uncomfortable feeling I was being followed and began to walk more rapidly. I noticed that there were hardly any people around. No matter how fast I walked, whoever was following me was keeping up with me. Finally, a lone figure came up beside me. I stood still and saw a wizened old, toothless gypsy woman. She wore colorful scarves around her neck and heavy gold earrings. In a loud voice, she yelled, 'Mira!'

"In a trembling voice, I said, 'What do you want?'

"'I want you to buy this.' The old gypsy woman reached into her satchel and pulled out a beautiful blue and white lace tablecloth and eight matching napkins.

"'Your tablecloth is beautiful,' I said. 'But I don't have enough money to pay for such a beautiful piece of work.'

"Her eyes flashed with anger. 'Give me what you have,' she said.

"I dug into my pockets. I had one ten-dollar bill. Nothing else!

"The gypsy eyed me suspiciously. I knew she thought that I had more money. I turned my pockets inside out. She saw to her dismay that ten dollars was all I had to offer her.

"With a furious gesture, she wrapped up the beautiful tablecloth and the eight napkins in newspaper and threw them at me. Then the gypsy vanished as quickly as she had appeared. Two hours later, I returned to the café to find my friends all looking worried.

"'Where have you been?' they asked me.

"I told them the story and unrolled the purchase. They gasped, saying, 'How did you ever get the gypsy to sell you such a beautiful prize for so little money?' I told them the story. They couldn't believe how lucky I was (nor could I)! The tablecloth and napkins are still in my possession. They are a favorite treasure!"

Andrea explains . . . "although Tanya had nothing to do with WW II she lived in those turbulent times."

Tanya is one of my favorite stories.

# Tanya of Russia:

## A Folklore Gem

"Hello! My name is Tatiana, but everyone calls me Tanya. I'm a doll, but even so, I'm feeling sad. You see, Babushka, which is what children in Russia call their grandmother, has been sitting on the same corner for many years just outside the city of Saint Petersburg, Russia. She's spent long hours and many years making dolls. As I am to be the last doll she will ever make, she is spending even more time making me.

"She often whispers to me, 'Little Tanya! Since you will be the last doll I'll ever make, I'll make sure you'll be the most beautiful of all my dolls. I've become too old, and I am almost blind. I have no more energy left to make dolls.'

"Shall I tell you a secret? Don't tell anyone. They won't believe you anyway—it sounds too crazy. I can't explain why, but I've always wanted to travel to meet new people and be with other dolls that are like me. What's upsetting? Well, for one thing, I've been sitting here on this corner watching all the tourists go by in big buses, on motorcycles, and in cars. I wonder where they're all going. I hope someone buys me. What's sad is that very few people seem to be interested in buying dolls anymore. Even though the family is poor, Babushka has decided to keep me for herself. I'm honored to be Babushka's 'favorite doll,' but I do so want to travel and see the world. I hope someone buys me. Would I miss Babushka and her family? I'm a doll. I honestly can't answer that question.

"Anyway, one day, a miracle took place. I suppose you'd call it a miracle. Babushka was about to finish putting the last stitches on my dress. A big bus suddenly stopped right in front of where we were sitting. The girls sitting by Babushka's side had also spent many long hours sitting on the corner with her. Sophia was Babushka's daughter. Anaya was Babushka's granddaughter. They were so devoted to her. Babushka never bothered to look up. She didn't notice the big bus, but I did! Babushka was determined to finish me that very day.

An American woman jumped off the bus and came over. She seemed to be around the same age as Sophia. She stood right in front of our doll stand and asked, "Do any of you speak English?"

Sophia answered shyly, "I speak a little English."

The woman smiled at Sophia. "My name is Andrea." She reached out her hand toward Sophia. "I would love to buy that doll," Andrea said, pointing toward me. "But first, please tell me your name."

Sophia responded in broken English, "My name—is Sophia." For a moment, two women from across the miles of ocean shook hands and smiled at one another.

"How much do you want for this beautiful doll?" Andrea repeated.

Sophia tapped her mother on her shoulder, and speaking in Russian, she told Babushka that the woman named "Andrea" wanted to buy me. She says she's started collecting dolls and would love to buy Tanya and take her to her country. She wants to know how much you want for her.

Without looking up, Babushka shook her head. "I'm not finished making the doll" was all the old Babushka said.

Then Sophia pointed to the youngest girls and said, "This is Anaya."

Anaya suddenly spoke up, "We can't sell Babushka's dolls without her permission. This is the last doll she'll ever make. We're sorry. This doll is not for sale." She was speaking in rapid Russian. I didn't understand a word.

"To continue my story, it's a good thing I'm just a doll and can't show any emotion. I'm sure my expression would have proved how crushed I was feeling."

Andrea said to Sophia, "Please tell your grandmother I'll pay whatever she wants for that lovely doll." The tourists on the bus were getting restless. Since Andrea didn't speak Russian, she knew she would have to go away without me. Never had she felt so dejected. She knew the Russian doll belonged in her doll collection. Andrea thanked them and began to walk toward the bus.

All of a sudden, Sophia called out, "Wait, please. Come back tomorrow. Maybe Babushka will change her mind."

The next morning was to be the last day of the group tour in Saint Petersburg. They were to leave the city at four in the afternoon, but Andrea couldn't get the doll out of her mind. She didn't sleep at all that night. She waited by the hotel lobby hoping to find her tour guide, Peggy Coleman. By midday, she saw her walking across the long hall and begged her to go back with her to Babushka's doll stand. Luckily, Peggy spoke fluent Russian, but she seemed puzzled that anyone could be so passionate about a doll.

"Can you tell me you actually remember where the doll stand is?" Peggy asked, looking amazed.

"Yes, I can. I took down the directions," said Andrea.

Now armed with a Russian-speaking friend, Andrea felt as though she could conquer the world. Everyone asked them where they were going. It seemed to Andrea that Peggy had decided to ignore the question, although she was not at all sure why. She gave some vague answer, and off they went. After a few wrong turns, they finally found the stand. To Andrea's great relief, the two girls were there. They were packing up the rest of the unsold dolls, but the doll Andrea wanted to buy was nowhere in sight. She felt her heart sink. Maybe someone else had come by and bought her. As they approached, Andrea suddenly saw old Babushka bending over. She was holding her hand over her heart, and she was obviously in pain.

Peggy, speaking in Russian, asked, "Would you like us to take your grandmother to the hospital? The taxi is nearby."

The girls shook their heads. "No, thank you. Our brother will be coming soon."

Then Peggy began talking rapidly to the girls. Andrea felt sure that whatever she was asking them was in order to distract the two worried girls until their brother arrived, but Andrea had to wait until later to hear what the question was all about.

Peggy had asked, "Would you please remind me of the story of how young children are taught about the long, icy-cold winters in Russia and the challenges men have to face when they have to travel to their jobs outside of the city?"

Sophia said, "Yes, Anaya and I can both tell you that story." Anaya had her arm around Babushka.

"You see," Sophia began, "children are told that wolves hunt people who come anywhere near the frozen tundra. They are haunted by the stories of green-eyed and yellow-eyed wolves.

"The children often wake up screaming from their nightmares. They have terrible dreams of falling off a coach and being stuck in the snow. They say they can hear wolves howling in the silent night. They hear the wolves, but they never see them. The parents and grandparents believe these stories help children to deal with long, cold winters and hard times. Children are taught to pray for their fathers when they have to leave the city for whatever reason. They are taught to pray for every member of their family including themselves."

Anaya suddenly spoke, turning toward Peggy, "Please translate this story for your friend and explain how Babushka's entire family feels. You see, if Babushka dies, the family may starve. It's like hearing the story of the wolves all over again, so we just keep praying. None of our family is a master doll maker. None of us can take Babushka's place. Can you understand?"

Peggy shook her head in sorrow and said, "Da! What a sad story. We'll go now. We're sorry to have bothered you. Thank you for sharing the story. My friend will appreciate knowing it." Peggy took Andrea's arm.

Just as they approached the taxi, Sophia called out to Peggy, "Wait! Please wait! Babushka has changed her mind. She feels your friend will keep Tanya safe."

Years later, Andrea would remember these stories as she stood in her living room holding Tanya who appeared to be laughing.

"Andrea, I could see by your face what amazement you felt," said Tanya.

"Yes," Andrea answered. "I couldn't believe it!"

"As Peggy started leading me back to the doll stand, I saw Sophia reaching down to a low shelf. She pulled out a woven red-striped bag. I remember she opened the bag and handed it to me. Oh, how pleased I was! For there you were, resting peacefully inside the bag. You seemed to have a big smile on your face!"

"I smiled once more, remembering when Andrea first knew she would fight passionately for the sake of having a doll, and I, that very doll, would finally find a home that would be the best in the world."

"I remember you turned to your friend, Peggy, and said, 'Please ask Babushka if she's really sure she wants to sell this doll. If she says yes, tell her I promise to keep her doll safe. I will always keep her and her family in my prayers. I promise to tell the story of the wolves and how important they are in teaching Russian children about their country. I give doll lectures so our American children will learn about your country. I'm sure after hearing this story, they will want to learn more about Russia.'"

Andrea was collecting a lifetime of memories that she could think back upon—the dolls, the cold of Russia, Babushka clutching her chest, and the moment in the chill of that sunlit day in Russia on the sidewalk curb when she had wanted to give Babushka's family something very special in exchange for the beautiful doll.

She had opened her pocket book, pulled out double the amount of money the girls said was the correct price, and had written her name and address on a sheet of paper to hand to Sophia. Andrea wanted them both to know her name and where she lived.

She had gone over to Babushka, and kneeling beside her, she turned to look up at Peggy.

"Peggy! Please tell her what I'm saying."

Gazing back at Babushka, she said, "Thank you, thank you so much for trusting me with your beautiful doll. I will forever cherish her."

The old lady nodded and smiled her toothless smile. Andrea got up and turned to hug both Sophia and Anaya. As the taxi pulled away, she saw the women waving. Andrea felt her eyes tearing up as she looked at the brave little group standing on a corner where they had spent most of their lifetime helping their grandmother sell her dolls. Andrea felt a great relief as she saw another car arriving. She knew the brother had arrived and that Babushka would be cared for. She knew this would be a day she'd never forget.

# Macuda of Korea/ Philippines:

## An Extreme Sacrifice

A few years ago, a young woman from Hawaii came to spend two nights with Andrea. Her name was Sarah. She told Andrea she had been born in Korea. Andrea had assumed her nationality was Hawaiian. Sarah was well traveled. In Andrea's growing doll collection, there was a doll whose origins were unknown to her. She didn't know what country she came from. Knowing Sarah had been to many lands, Andrea asked her if she would look at this specific doll to see if she might know anything about her. Andrea started describing the beautiful doll to her.

"She wears a small crown perched at the front of her hairdo. She has dark eyes and wears a knowing smile. Long pearl earrings adorn her delicate ears and around her throat, like a choker.

"She has a necklace of pearls. The doll's left arm looks as though she's about to beat on the instrument she's holding. It's long handled and looks delicate. What country do you suppose she's from?"

"Oh, go get her!" Sarah said. "It sounds as though she could be from my country." Andrea handed the doll to Sarah. She took the doll in her hands, looking at it with great interest.

"You know, Andrea, I think this doll is from my country of Korea. If not from there, then perhaps she might be from the Philippines. I'm not quite sure, but I do recall that women in Korea often learned how to play music on just such a long-handled instrument. My family left Korea for Hawaii when I was still very young, so I never learned how to play any musical instrument. I bet this doll is named Macuda who lived in a village in North Korea known as Kijong-Dong. As legend has it, she lived a very sad life, although I do not remember why her life held such sadness."

Sarah carefully placed Macuda back on the doll shelf. Her visit had given Macuda the name of her country. Andrea was very grateful to her. They spent the rest of their visit together talking of travel and dolls from different parts of the world.

After Sarah left to return to Hawaii, Andrea took Macuda out of the glass doll cabinet and looked at her for a long time. Then she asked her, "Macuda! At last I know where you are from. I already know that your story is a sad one, but please, do tell your tragic tale in your own words."

Here is Macuda's story:

## MACUDA SPEAKS

"Andrea! I know you love me, even though I'm just one of the dolls in your large collection. So yes! I will tell you my story, and it is a true story!

"I lived in a small village in North Korea, just like Sarah told you called Kijong-Dong, with my father and my brother, Kim. In the language of our country, Macuda means gift! My father was old and blind. He was dependent upon me to do everything for him, including the cooking, washing of clothes, grocery, shopping, and keeping the house clean. We had very little money, and my brother and I knew that eventually, we'd have to find work. Every day, I played music with my brother. He was a talented drummer. I am a singer. I always teased my brother about his dropping of one note halfway through our ballad. We laughed a lot, but finally, we were forced to grow up. We were no longer children. We both realized that we had to get a job.

"Since my father had become blind, we had grown poorer than ever. Kim knew the owner of the local club. He often went there to meet with friends and refresh himself, hoping to forget the difficult situation since his father had become old and blind. Anyway, thanks to Kim, we were hired almost immediately and appeared every night except Sunday to play music. We became very popular.

"Father began to fear we would both leave him to fend for himself. He decided he would have to poison me, his only daughter, in order to keep me nearby. He began putting small lethal drops of poison in my tea. I watched him adding the drops of poison to everything I drank or ate. I knew what he was doing and why he was doing this hideous thing. I allowed him to poison me, knowing full well I'd soon become as blind as he was. When my brother discovered what my father was doing and that I had allowed it, he became furious. He told me I was a stupid girl and that if I became completely blind, he would leave and never return home. I wept and begged him to understand, but he paid no heed.

"Soon, I was all alone caring for my father. I knew every inch of my father's house and continued caring for him, even though my eyesight was fading with each passing day. Soon I found myself totally blind. I needed no eyesight though, for I had memorized every corner of the club's stage and my dressing room. I had no problem walking every night to the club to sing. I had done it so many times. Only one thing had changed. I was now told I had to sing every night including Sundays, with or without my brother, and that the last song always had to be the same. It was a heartbreaking song of a beautiful young woman who was slowly blinded by her father and then left, not by a lover as in the song but by her brother to take care of the old, senile, blind father.

"It was a favorite ballad of many. No one knew that I was singing about my own tragic tale. No one knew that I was totally blind. Not one member of the audience would leave until they had heard my last song. I always sang that song at the end of my repertoire. Then everyone would stand and cheer and clap. The owner knew this song was his best bet for good business.

"After several months had passed, I decided I couldn't sing that sad song anymore. I needed my brother, and he wasn't there. I told the owner I would continue to play but that I could not sing that song again. He became very irate.

"'Macuda!' he shouted, 'if you don't sing that song, I'll fire you! It's the most popular ballad in your repertoire. You have to sing it!'

"I just hid in the back room and cried. I knew I couldn't give up the job. We were too poor. I needed my brother to play his fabulous drums. It just so happened on that particular night, a stranger came to town. I did not know it then, but it was Kim. His intention was to visit the club one more time. He wanted to catch up with his old friends before leaving his village forever. He'd heard there was an incredible singer at the club, and as he was sure I would be at home taking care of Father, he thought he'd see if the new singer was half as good as his sister. He planned to depart that same evening without seeing either his father or me.

"The owner of the club recognized Kim immediately. His face lit up. 'I'm so glad to see you, Kim!' he said. 'Your sister refuses to sing her famous ballad anymore. She's in the back room crying. I told her I would fire her if she didn't sing that song tonight. It is the favorite one for the audience. No one ever leaves the club until she sings that last song. It's very good for business. I'm sure you understand.'

"'Tell your singer to come and sing,' said Kim. 'Tell her a famous musician has agreed to accompany her for the last ballad.'

Macuda paused for a moment in her story. Then she continued.

"You can understand, I had no choice. I had to play or be fired. I walked slowly onto the stage. Kim told me later how shocked he was to see how thin and pale I had become.

"'Strangely,' he later told me, 'you have become even more beautiful than ever.'

"The show went on, and I sang many songs that night. The stranger with the drums sat silently in the back, far and away from the stage. Finally, it was time for my last song. As I began to sing, the drummer started his rhythmic beat. Somewhere in the middle of the song, the drummer dropped a note. My heart stopped! But my voice was strong. I knew who the drummer was, and my tears of sadness turned to tears of joy. My beloved brother was here playing his drums to my song. When the song ended, everyone in the audience stood up as 'one' and clapped and cheered for a long, long time. That night, we went home hand in hand, rejoicing to be together again at last.

"'Can you stay for a few days, dear brother?' I asked.

"He leaned over and kissed me on my forehead and whispered, 'Have no fear, Macuda! I have been selfish. If you'll forgive me for being selfish and leaving you alone to take care of our father, I promise to stay with you always. Now I understand why you wouldn't leave our father. I also promise to forgive father. You were God's gift to him. I will never leave you or Father alone again.'"

The actual doll, Yumi, remained with Mrs. Dickinson. This is a painting of Yumi. Photo courtesy of Hiroko Okahashi.

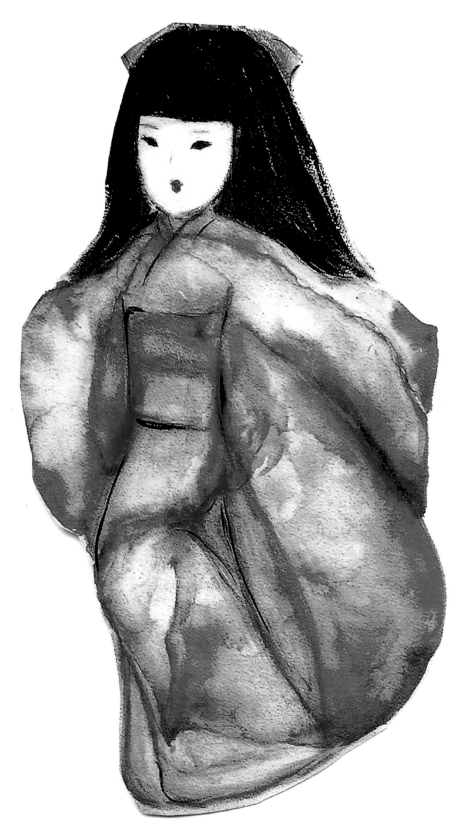

The actual doll, Yumi remained with Mrs.
Dickinson.  This is a painting of Yumi.
*Photo courtesy of Hiroko  Okahashi.*

# Yumi of Japan:

## A Spy's Good-luck Doll

People say, "Dolls are not human. They have no emotions." Of course, this is not true! What most people don't realize is that dolls have stories to tell that are not only unique but also absolutely true and historically interesting! I'll tell you a secret. If someone believes that a doll is precious, oftentimes that is enough to make something magic happen. Why? Because the owner will always keep that doll close by, for it will forever remain a good-luck doll. No other doll will ever be able to take their place. That's what happened a long time ago.

One day, Mrs. Dickinson, the famous doll collector from New York City, exhibiting all her greatest charms, walked into a doll shop in Nagano, Japan, and introduced herself.

"Mr. Magaburo! My name is Velvalee Dickinson. I've been told you are one of the finest doll makers in Japan. I'm interested in buying one of your dolls. Would you show me your collection, please? I have an extensive collection myself and never stop looking for more dolls to add to my collection."

"Indeed!" said Mr. Magaburo. "My pleasure! You are well known as a collector. It's an honor to meet you. Please! Follow me!"

Mrs. Dickinson extended her slender white-gloved hand, but Mr. Magaburo simply bowed and began walking slowly up a long, curving, narrow flight of stairs.

"This way, please," he said as he led the way. Mrs. Dickinson followed, but as she turned the corner of the hall, she passed a closet with a sheer white curtain. She couldn't resist peeking. Gently, she raised the curtain. A beautiful Japanese doll was staring intently at her. She had never seen a lovelier doll and knew she had to have her at any price. She also knew that Mr. Magaburo had stopped halfway up the stairs and was waiting for her to follow him to his upstairs room where he kept his many beautiful dolls. As soon as they entered the room upstairs, Mrs. Dickinson wasted no time.

"Mr. Magaburo," she said, "would you consider selling the lovely Japanese doll that I happened to see hiding behind the curtain downstairs?"

Mr. Magaburo looked upset. He replied stiffly. "I'm sorry, Mrs. Dickinson, but that doll has just been completed, and I'm not prepared to sell her yet. Won't you please consider another doll?"

She replied, "I can't do that! I know a good-luck doll when I see one. She is definitely going to be my good-luck doll! I must have her. And that's all there is to it! I will pay you any price you request. Any price at all!"

Mr. Magaburo could not believe his ears. How could she know his special Yumi was a good-luck doll? He had planned to make the doll his good-luck doll.

"I don't know. I don't know." He looked sad as he muttered these words. "I gave her the name Yumi and plan on keeping her," he said quietly.

"Mr. Magaburo, as I've already mentioned, you may name your price. Any price! I promise I'll take very good care of Yumi."

There was a long silence as Mr. Magaburo thought about Yumi. He didn't want to sell her at all, but then he thought about his ailing father who needed medical care. He had promised himself that with the sale of the very next doll, he'd spend it all on getting his sick father the best treatment he could. He knew he had to remain true to his promise. With an agonizing sigh, he made the painful decision to give Mrs. Dickinson the doll for the high price she was willing to pay. Walking slowly down the stairs, Mr. Magaburo hesitated for one brief moment before he pulled back the curtain.

"Yumi," he whispered, "forgive me. You know how much I love you." Gently, he lifted the doll out; and with great care, he wrapped and handed her to Mrs. Dickinson.

She grabbed the doll after paying a handsome price for her, and barely thanking the old doll maker, she ran out of the store clutching Yumi in a tight death grip.

"You will come with me wherever I go, Yumi," said Mrs. Dickinson. "You'll meet interesting people all over America. You will always be my good-luck doll."

Yumi was feeling torn between two emotions. On the one hand, she felt sad for Mr. Magaburo. On the other hand, she was excited to become a good-luck doll for a famous doll collector. At this point, Yumi decided to tell the story in her own words. She began to speak.

## YUMI SPEAKS

"At last I have the chance to travel to America. Mrs. Dickinson kept her word. We met fascinating people everywhere, but her favorite place seemed to be San Francisco. Whenever she came to town, the doors of many houses would fly open. We were received like royalty. It was interesting to see the large doll collections these women had collected. Many dolls were from Japan—my country. Everyone insisted I was the most beautiful of all the Japanese dolls. I think I felt pleased, but I can't be sure. Several of the women asked to buy me, but Mrs. Dickinson refused every request in her charming way. Many of those ladies later came to New York City and paid good prices for other international dolls in Mrs. Dickinson's collection. But I was never for sale!

"One day, Mr. Dickinson appeared. He went to the closet to hang up his coat.

"'My dear,' he said, 'why is the gypsy doll stuffed in the back of this closet? Do you really despise her so much that you punish her and throw her into the closet?'

"'I don't want that doll in my collection!' Mrs. Dickinson shrieked. 'Don't you understand? She's too ugly.'

"'But, my dear,' replied her husband, 'remember that gypsies can be one's best friend or a daunting enemy. So treat her with affection, and she will bring you good luck and lots of money.'

"'She's too ugly, I tell you! She doesn't belong in my collection of beautiful dolls. You keep her! I don't want her! Take her away! Besides, her eyes are not real Mexican black pearls, as you always insist, but cheap glass!'

"Perla's bandana around her hair was all askew. Her eyes were sparkling black pools of ink. Mr. Dickinson carefully placed Perla into a chair and left. As soon as he was gone, Mrs. Dickinson jumped up and snatching Perla out of the rocking chair. She threw her back in the closet and slammed the door. Then she took me in her arms and placed me on her lap where we rocked in silence. As Mrs. Dickinson held me, I started thinking about Perla locked away behind that closet door. In some ways, I wished that Mr. Dickinson had never brought Perla into the doll shop. At first meeting Perla, I was frightened. She kept glaring at me as though she hated me.

"I returned those looks of hers with a smile. I wanted to comfort Mrs. Dickinson, but I didn't know how to do that. I realized she was a very smart woman but lonely in spite of her loving husband and all her adoring customers. I seemed to know she needed someone or something to comfort her. I am the something she needed."

From the darkness of the closet, an extreme sense of loneliness overcame Perla. She was beginning to wish she had never left her country. How she longed to be back with her loving Mexican family. The woman who came every week to clean the store appeared. Mrs. Dickinson asked her to hand her the red jacket from the closet.

"Mrs. Dickinson," said the woman, sounding shocked, "did you know there is a doll lying on the floor in the closet?"

Mrs. Dickinson snapped, "Just hand me my jacket."

As soon as Mrs. Dickinson left the shop, the cleaning lady, feeling sympathy for the gypsy doll, took the doll out, dusted her off, and placed her on an empty shelf in the back of the room.

When she'd finished straightening the place, she turned to both dolls and gave them a wink.

Then wagging her finger at Perla, she said with a big smile, "You better behave yourself, you hear?" She turned and closed the door behind her.

Feeling grateful for having been rescued from the bottom of the dusty closet, Perla felt brave enough to start a conversation with Yumi. She wanted to reveal to Yumi all she knew about Mrs. Dickinson's secret life. From across the room, she began speaking to Yumi. With her gypsy's intuition, she quietly thought to herself, There's more than meets the eye with Yumi. I know she still doesn't trust me, but in time she will. I feel sure we will end up being friends.

Then Perla explained to Yumi, "I not only see all the people who come to visit. I hear what they're saying. I hear the frightening plan Mrs. Dickinson is about to undertake. She is going to work for Japan instead of working for America."

"Yes, I know that," said Yumi. "But I can't understand why there are such bad feelings between Japan and the United States. All I know is that Mrs. Dickinson never thinks of the Japanese people as her enemies. They've always been her friends. She worked for them in the Imperial Valley as a CEO. They paid her a handsome salary to get information from other doll collectors. The company always treats her with respect. They know how brilliant and dedicated she is. She is as pleased with them as they are with her."

"Ah, si. I've heard that before," Perla replied.

Yumi thought to herself, I'll let Perla think she knows everything. It's true! Gypsies have powers to see things that most others might miss. So I might as well take Perla into my confidence.

Yumi continued, "One afternoon, Mrs. Dickinson's boss asked her to come into his office. She wondered if she'd done something wrong."

"'Do sit down, Mrs. Dickinson,' he said.

"The commander wore a white uniform with gold brass and matching buttons. He was an impressive-looking man. Mrs. Dickinson knew the officer was an extremely important naval commander in the Japanese Navy.

"'What do you want me to do, sir?' she asked nervously. She sat down primly and waited to hear what was on her boss's mind.

"'I have an offer to make you, Mrs. Dickinson. It won't be an easy job, but it will be an exciting one. It will bring you a considerably larger salary than you are receiving now. We know you'd be the perfect person to handle it.' The commander then explained in detail what the job would entail.

"'If you choose to accept the offer, you will be introduced to our entire staff this afternoon at precisely four in the afternoon. I assure you everyone will be very pleased to hear you'll be joining our team. Might you be interested, Mrs. Dickinson?'

"Mrs. Dickinson said, 'Thank you, sir, I'd be delighted to help you in any way I can. I accept your offer with pleasure. It sounds challenging, but I love challenges. Besides, I have to make more money to take care of my poor husband. He is very ill.'

"'Then it's a deal, Mrs. Dickinson. Glad to have you on board.' The commander stood up and opened the door for Mrs. Dickinson to leave.

"'Wait! Wait!' shouted Perla. 'This is an interesting story, Yumi. What job does the Japanese commander offer to Mrs. Dickinson?'"

Yumi feels Perla's hypnotic eyes looking at her, and taking but a moment, she responds, "Mrs. Dickinson is offered the job of contacting old and new doll customers in the San Francisco area. She is thrilled with the idea. She figures this is a great way to find new customers to buy her dolls. But first, she must find out what type of ships, submarines, and planes are going to come into Pearl Harbor and the time they will be arriving. It doesn't seem to be too much of a daunting job. It sounds like fun to her."

Perla, now totally drawn in by Yumi's story, says, "Do continue."

Yumi answers, "My owner is so smart. She decides to get in touch with one of her best customers, a Mrs. Hooker, who is delighted to invite the famous doll collector to tea. She has several Dickinson dolls in her collection.

"Mrs. Dickinson plunges right in, asking her hostess to tell her all about her husband—where he is and when he'll be home. She asks, 'What part of the Navy is your husband in?'

"Mrs. Hooker has no reason to be concerned about Mrs. Dickinson's question. She tells her everything.

"After gleaning all the necessary information, she gets up to leave. She asks her hostess if there is another doll collector in the area or anywhere else around San Francisco. Mrs. Hooker immediately provides an address and a phone number of a good friend. With that, Mrs. Dickinson takes leave, giving her hostess a warm hug.

"She then scurries back to an out-of-the-way small hotel and begins writing a letter to her new contact. In her own handwriting, she writes, 'I just had a lovely tea with a dear friend, and I took the liberty of giving her your address and phone number. I know you will enjoy meeting her. You have a lot in common. She's longing to see your doll collection. She'll be in touch with you soon. Your old friend, Anne Hooker.'

"'Yumi,' says Perla, 'you know perfectly well that Mrs. Dickinson has no problem copying handwriting. She's an expert forger.'"

Yumi says, "Perla, believe me, the doors always fly open for Mrs. Dickinson. If the person hasn't met her, it makes no difference. Her dolls are famous, and so is she. Over tea, Mrs. Dickinson listens sympathetically to the wives telling how much they miss their dear husbands. The ladies feel Mrs. Dickinson is a sweet person and is so well educated. She impresses everyone. The wives always tell her of the whereabouts of their husbands and what kind of vessel or plane they are on.

"You know, Perla," says Yumi, "Mrs. Dickinson did a very good job gathering information."

Yumi hesitates for a moment as though she isn't quite sure she should go on. She decides to change the subject.

In a dreamy voice, Yumi says, "Isn't it wonderful that Mrs. Dickinson came all the way to Japan just to find me? She tells everyone I am her good-luck doll. I feel lucky that she loves me so much. She never goes anywhere without me."

Suddenly, Perla blurts out, "You may not want to hear this, Yumi, but I'm sure your owner is a traitor. I heard her tell her Japanese boss she'd write letters to a contact by the name of Señora Molinari in Buenos Aires, Argentina, telling her about her dolls. Dolls is a secret code for battleship. That's what her boss tells her. He says, Write to Señora Molinari that three English dolls will soon be in your possession. English dolls translate into a secret code called props. For example, the fisherman with a net over his shoulder is very important. Fishing nets stands for subs protecting the harbor. The old woman with the wood piled on her back, as well as the elderly gentleman doll holding a basket of fresh vegetables, are all used as descriptive codes that will tell the Japanese three important ships of war are in the San Francisco port for repairs and fittings. One of the letters say, Mr. Shaw has been very ill, so the trip to Louisville has been canceled. Mr. Shaw refers to the destroyer Shaw Louisville. French dolls mean some of the French fleets in various American ports. Balloons represent other coastal defense installations."

Perla stops to take a breath.

"I can also tell you how the FBI finally catches up to your owner—a spy!"

Yumi shouts, "No, don't go on, Perla. I hear what you're saying, but I'm here to be Mrs. Dickinson's good-luck doll. I do remember one incident, however." She pauses briefly.

"Tell me, please tell me," says Perla.

"All right, I will tell you what happened. We were on a train returning to New York City from San Francisco. The conductor came by to collect the train ticket. When he saw me, he began asking questions," said Yumi. "My owner was very tired. She hates being asked questions by strangers. She was very rude to the conductor. The conductor thought he might have seen this strange woman before, but he couldn't remember where. He left her alone without questioning her further. Mrs. Dickinson was relieved. She lay back in her seat, and holding me close, she closed her eyes and fell fast asleep.

"Back in the city, Mrs. Dickinson decided to sell all her dolls except me. She then decided to take every penny of her money out of the bank vault and return to California to find her boss. Poor Mrs. Dickinson! She was caught in the bank vault and hustled off to face her trial as a spy and a traitor. She narrowly escaped being electrocuted. For a long time, no one knew what had happened to the famous doll collector. The reason was because the judges didn't want the Japanese to know that their number one spy had been caught."

"I'm sorry you had to go through all of this, Yumi," said Perla softly. "I've known about Mrs. Dickinson's activities for a long time. You weren't ready to hear it."

Yumi ignored the remark.

Turning toward Perla, she said, "Those were ten of the longest, loneliest years for us both. I know how much my owner suffered. I'm sure I learned the meaning of sadness during those bleak years."

Perla interrupted her and asked, "Do you think there can ever be redemption for Mrs. Dickinson?"

Yumi was silent for a long time. Then she spoke. "I could make many prayers and wishes for my dear tortured owner, but for now, my hope is that she opens her heart to take away the darkness and let in the light so that she can finally learn the true meaning of love."

## More Than Meets the Eye

• • • • • • • • • • • • • • • • • • •

Many years later, all the dolls are gathered in the living room of their new owner, Andrea. The sun is streaming through the windows, and Perla's eyes are sparkling. Had you been watching? You might have seen Perla nodding and smiling at Yumi, and Yumi smiling back.

The dolls wait until nightfall when all are sleeping. They will have a celebration for Perla and Yumi who have, at long last, become best friends.

*Fuji Mountain with Fuji Flower*

# Akira of Japan:

## A Terrifying Tale

It was Andrea's grandfather who gave Andrea her first doll. He had taken a year-long trip around the world with his son, Jimmy, returning one wonderful day in late August. They walked into the living room as though they had just come in from a swim at the beach club or a game of tennis at the Meadow Club. Andrea was twelve years old. She would never forget the joy of that moment. Her grandfather hugged her, saying, "Bibby,"—that was his favorite name for her—"I've bought you a special gift from Japan. Do you see that large box in the hallway? That's for you. Go ahead and open it, but be careful. It's very heavy." Andrea rushed into the hall and began tearing open the box. Her grandfather had to help her.

She couldn't imagine what would come out of such a huge box. She was very excited. The gift was finally revealed. Inside a glass case was a strange-looking doll. Andrea's face fell. Why had her grandfather bought her a doll? He knew perfectly well she had no interest whatsoever in dolls.

It was certainly magnificent to look at. Andrea was quite awestruck, but the doll made her feel uncomfortable. It was as though she was hiding something personal that she didn't want to share with anyone.

Andrea got a spooky feeling that the doll might have been a man dressed like a woman.

The doll wore a long, flowing kimono and carried three large red hats in each hand, with a similar tilted hat on her black hair. Andrea thought the hats looked more like umbrellas or big plates.

She was confused by the gift and tried to thank her grandfather properly. Instead, she blurted out, "Thanks! But that case is too heavy for me to lift. Could you stick that doll somewhere up on a high shelf, please?"

Her grandfather wasn't in the least bit surprised by her reaction. He smiled, saying, "Someday, Bibby, when you're a little older, you'll realize how valuable this doll really is. She is a Kabuki dancer." He then took the case with the doll and placed it in the bamboo room on a high shelf.

For many years, the beautiful doll lived on high shelves without being given much attention by anyone, including, for that matter, Andrea.

Andrea's grandfather came home with unusual gifts from Japan and China. He'd become particularly interested in Asian culture. One of the most interesting gifts was a rather large porcelain Buddha from China. He claimed he needed the Buddha at the dining room table because his extensive, noisy family was often too busy eating and talking. Their grandfather was also at the table sharing a meal. His wife would say, "Oh really, Jim! Do you have to play with a toy at the dinner table? You should be talking with your grandchildren." He'd say, "My dear, this Buddha is not a toy. He's become my close friend. When no one talks to me, the Buddha and I have fascinating discussions together. He always listens to me, which is more than can be said for the rest of the folk around the table." Andrea's grandmother would drop the subject, knowing full well she'd get nowhere with her husband.

Each night, Andrea's grandfather would place the Buddha in front of him. When he felt as if he needed to be listened to, he'd push down the head of the Buddha, who would then nod at him and stick out his tongue. Andrea didn't like the Buddha. Something about the Buddha scared her, but that's another story for another time.

Years later, when Andrea had collected many fascinating dolls from around the world, she began to lecture with the dolls at schools, libraries, international fairs, hospitals, and private homes for children's birthday parties. Several times, she took the Kabuki dancer in the heavy case to show her off. The Japanese doll was magnificent to look at, but it wasn't until later that Andrea began to study and find out all that she could about Kabuki dancers. Finally, she had to stop taking the doll with her to lectures. She was just too cumbersome in her glass case for Andrea to carry around.

It was now time for Akira to tell her story in her own words, but because Andrea had left the doll behind so often, the doll felt abandoned and didn't want to speak to anyone. When asked to tell her story, Akira refused to speak. All the dolls began to shout.

"Please, please! Talk to us, Akira. We want to hear you tell your story. You've been silent and locked away in your glass case for too long."

In unison, all the dolls cried out, "We really, really care! Please tell us your story now!"

Slowly, the doll began to tell her story.

## AKIRA SPEAKS

My name is Akira. In Japanese, Akira means intelligent. Akira is both a girl's name and a boy's name but chiefly used as the name of a male. As an only son, my parents wanted the best for me. The name of Akira, they told me, was appropriate. I had always been an excellent student.

On most nights, our family ate dinner around 6:00 p.m., and then we went to different rooms to read, study, or sleep. One day, something surprising happened. My father approached me in the afternoon, saying, "Son, tonight we are preparing a feast in your honor. You will be the guest of honor." I was stunned.

"Why is that so?" I asked my father.

"It is to celebrate your future," he replied.

"My future?" I asked.

• • • • • • • • • • • • • • • • • • • •

"Yes, your future," said my father. "Your mother and I, with approval from your grandparents, have decided where you will be going to school. You will hear more tonight."

I asked, "A dinner in my honor? I am only twelve years old!"

In my mind, I had already planned that I'd be going to school with my friends who, like me, were enthusiastic sports fans. Something didn't feel right, and as dinnertime approached, I became more and more agitated. But my nose told me that whatever was planned, the dinner would be a memorable one. It wasn't until the end of a superb meal that I was to hear what fate had been planned for me. My father cleared his throat and began to speak.

"Your mother and I have decided to send you to the most exclusive school in all of Tokyo and Kyoto. It is a school where boys are taught Kabuki dancing. Kabuki dancing is the most highly respected art in all of Japan and the world. The dances started in the sixteenth century."

"But, Father, I can't dance!"

"You will learn" was my father's response.

"What kind of dance must I learn, Father?"

"The dance trains young men your age to be like women in every way. You will learn how to move like a woman and dress like a woman in exquisite costumes. Costumes must be changed more than once during the dance. You will be a wonderful Kabuki dancer, Akira, and make us, your grandparents, and friends very proud of you."

I felt like crying, but boys don't cry. One thing I knew for sure, like it or not, I was to go to a Kabuki school and be a Kabuki dancer for the rest of my life. And most of all, I could not entertain the thought of failing, for failing in Japan causes shame. Often, shame means only one thing: hara-kiri—the taking of one's own life. A week later, my father accompanied me to my new school. As we left the house, a group of friends gathered outside. I didn't want to look at them for fear of crying.

Soon after arriving at the school, because of my own anger and despair, I began studying to see which dance might be the most frightening and difficult to perform. I thought that it might help ease my own fury at my fate. In school, we learned that to become a Kabuki dancer, it would take five to seven years before we would be allowed to perform. The more I learned about Kabuki dancing, the more fascinated I became. I loved the hauntingly beautiful Nagato music. In the Japanese Kabuki schools, the music is one of the most important parts of the rituals of the dances.

At last, one of my dreams was coming true—listening to that amazing music.

Then one day, we were told a story about how Kabuki first came into being in the Edo era from 1603 to 1868. It was not performed until 1826 and only as one dance in a series of five dances.

When the story of Fuji Musume, the Wisteria Maiden, was presented, I was entranced and decided I wanted to be the one to perform that dance. The Wisteria Maiden was one of the greatest of all challenges to perform. The maiden had to use difficult poses to show her emotions, which I could see myself performing. I was sad when I wasn't chosen to be the

Fuji Musume, but let me tell you the story. It satisfied another one of my dreams—that of becoming a painter.

As the story is told, there was a time, long ago, when a painter came to look at all the paintings that lined the street in a beautiful city called Otsu, outside of Kyoto. All the paintings were lovely, but one painting in particular caught his eye. He couldn't stop gazing at the beautiful, sad-looking maiden in the painting. She was dressed in a long, flowing kimono and carrying a bunch of gorgeous Fuji. The Wisteria Maiden became infatuated with the stranger gazing at her with such intensity. So much so that she came to life and stepped out of the painting. She found a pine tree covered in wisteria and began to dance for her lost love. Her admirer could see how sad she was. It was obvious to him that the beautiful Wisteria Maiden was heartbroken. He questioned a bystander and was told that her lover had returned all her love letters. The stranger reached out to console her. Without looking at him, she stepped back into the painting, where she will remain forever.

The story of the Wisteria Maiden enchanted me because, although most people don't know this, I have a soft heart. So of course, this story captivated my imagination. I found it wonderful, but I knew it would never be able to rid me of my anger and frustration. That's why I decided to ask permission to perform the dance called Dojoji. This is a frightening story, but it suited my temperament. I knew it was the dance that I needed to do in order to heal my troubled soul.

Six years later, I had learned a great deal about the Kabuki dancer who dances with six hats. The hats become the scales of a dreadful serpent. The dancer transforms into a demon of jealousy. This dance is called the Maiden at Dojoji temple. A young girl is asked to dance in the temple in honor of the raising of a new bell. As she begins the dance, she becomes enthralled with a young priest. At first sight, she falls passionately in love with him. However, the priest resists her charms and flees, hiding under the temple bell. She transforms into a serpent. As a serpent, she wraps herself around the bell and breathing out fire, burns the young priest to death.

I studied that dance for a long time. I was sure I could perform it. I'd never told anyone how I really felt about becoming a Kabuki dancer. The night my father informed me I was going to be sent to Kabuki school, my rage and despair, though hidden, almost got out of control. I showed no emotion, but I was enraged. Later on, I realized that my parents' choice for me to become a Kabuki dancer was the right choice. Life is so strange with its twists and turns.

Up to this point, the dolls had all been quiet, listening to Akira tell her story. You could have heard a pin drop in the silence that followed as the dolls waited for her to finish. It was a hot July night, and there was tension in the air. The dolls watched as their owner, Andrea, lifted Akira's glass case down from the high shelf. She placed the case next to her on the sofa and began speaking to the doll.

"Akira, by now you must know how beautiful and important you are." There was a silence. Akira had her back turned away from Andrea.

"After being on a high shelf all these years, you might think that I have neglected you," Andrea continued. "Let me explain what happened. Do you remember the young blonde girl that use to accompany me to my doll lectures? Do you remember that it was that girl who carried you with such care into classrooms, libraries, and women's clubs? I hardly ever left you behind, until my helper had to leave me. Your glass case was too heavy for me to carry. I always felt sad when I had to leave you behind. I hope you realize that now and have forgiven me."

Slowly, Akira turned around in her glass case and gazed at Andrea.

"Akira," said Andrea, "you are in your own glass universe. We can't take you out. Remember the dance of the Wisteria Maiden who stepped out of the painting to greet the stranger? She thought she could step into another world. She couldn't do it, and neither can you, dear Akira."

"I know," said Akira, finally speaking. "But it doesn't make it any less painful to feel sometimes as though I am trapped in a prison of my own."

All the dolls had been listening intently to Akira's story.

"You know, Akira," said Perla, "each of us has had our challenges. When I found out that I was not Andrea's first doll, but the second doll in her collection, I felt angry and jealous. I swore I'd never be your friend. Now that I have heard your story, I am no longer angry or jealous. I know what it's like to be hated. My former owner despised me. I beg you to forgive me."

"I forgive you, Perla," said Akira. "I know what it's like to live with resentment."

Andrea was sure she heard a sigh of relief from Perla.

"Please let me share some of my feelings," said Kasha. "Having come so close to being buried in the mud forever outside that death camp, I understand your feelings of despair. I'm afraid I have been selfish. It wasn't that I didn't like you. I just never thought about you because you were always so far above us. Your story moved me greatly. Let's be friends forever."

"Of course, Kasha, let's be friends forever," said Akira.

"You know," said Macuda, "I don't think everyone understands how hard it is to be selfless. I lived to keep my father safe and even went blind for him. Selflessness is sometimes taken for stupidity. Akira! By forgiving us, your understanding and empathy shows us the pathway to real love."

"I'm proud to know you, Macuda," said Akira. "You've been more than courageous throughout your life. The love for your father and your own passion to sing made you selfless. I'm sure it was a very lonely life for you. You've taught us that selflessness is sharing—you've shown us through a life of sacrifice and pain that you have never stopped loving. You live in the realm of light."

"Let's remember," said Perla, "the lessons we've learned are important. And now let's thank each other in our own language."

"What a wonderful idea!" said all the dolls in unison. "Why don't you begin, Perla?" said Akira.

Perla said, "Muy bien. Thank you in Spanish is gracias. And, Lita, you also speak Spanish."

"Ah, me gusta," said Lita. "Me gusta la idea. Gracias!" Lita interrupted enthusiastically. "Si, gracias is the same everywhere in Latin countries. Now it's your turn, Tanya."

"In Russia," said Tanya, "thank you is spasibo. Your turn, Macuda."

"All right," said Macuda. "In my country, we say, 'Kamsanida.' You're next, Kasha. Please spell 'thank you' for us in Polish."

Kasha softly answered, "I'll spell it. Are you ready? D-z-i-e-k-u-j-e."

"My turn," said Yumi. She looked at Akira. "We're lucky we both speak Japanese, aren't we, Akira? Why don't you tell everyone how we say thank you in Japanese?"

Akira said, "Yes, I will do that, Yumi. Thank you in Japanese is domo arigato."

"Now," said Andrea, gently lifting Akira and placing her on the coffee table, "you don't always have to live up on that high shelf."

"Oh, how delightful!" said Silly Lita, clapping her hands. "Now we can see you, Akira."

All the dolls thanked Andrea.

As she turned to leave, Andrea took one last look at her beloved dolls and whispered, "I'm sure someday you all will be recognized and loved as much as I love you."

Had you been around, you might have heard Akira whispering back, "Thank you, Andrea, for giving us such a happy home. We love you too."

When Andrea left the room, the dolls all agreed that from now on, July 13 would become their traditional day of celebration. It would become a joyous tradition of all that had brought them together. They would forever celebrate their individual dreams of finally being in a family and of overcoming their hardships and to celebrate, above all, their differences. This was the coming together of a true family.

. . . . . . . . . . . . . . . . . . . .

# EPILOGUE

Most of my doll collection stories are based on true stories of children who grew up in the forties and fifties. The children were born in different parts of the world, but they all had one thing in common. They loved their dolls unconditionally and often felt they were more real than the people around them. The courage of young people growing up in the shadows of World War II never left the mind of this collector. That's the reason why, after so many years, I decided to write these unusual, true, historic doll stories.

The most delightful discovery about being a doll owner is the knowledge that children, who have been brought together because of their dolls, overcome their differences. I witnessed that there was no separation between cultures among the children themselves. Oftentimes, these children grew up being spared a bitter heart and grew up pursuing love instead of hatred. I wasn't meant to be a doll collector, or so I thought.

After meeting Mrs. Dickinson, I certainly had no desire to ever become a doll collector. I had nightmares about her for years. I was totally traumatized from my experience of her. The day of confronting pure rage from a woman I had never met before shocked me severely. When she grabbed the doll from my hands and went off swinging the doll upside down by one leg, I made my very first vow—I would rescue the Mexican gypsy doll from that fiendish woman.

With me, I was sure the doll would be safe. I was still to hear that hissing, threatening voice and the rapid click-click of those red high-heeled shoes as the angry woman vanished rapidly down the bookstore aisles. The nightmares caused me to have severe headaches for a long time.

What a surprise to later discover that I hadn't chosen Perla but that she had chosen me.

She made me aware that I had grown up in a totally white world. It was not only the tall travel books that had caught my attention at the bookstore window but also Perla's dark complexion that told me how little I knew about other cultures. She was to change the course of my life forever.

Mrs. Dickinson had Yumi as her good-luck doll. When I finished writing these stories, I realized, for the first time, that I too had a good-luck doll. Perla has always been my good-luck doll and will remain so forever.

# ABOUT THE AUTHOR

Lee Lawrence was born in New York City and has been a resident of Cambridge since 1962. She has been writing since she was a child, penning several short stories, poetry, and plays.

Her first play, Tea and Tyranny, was a multimedia pageant presented in Cambridge, Massachusetts, in 1976 for the purpose of bringing history to life for the bicentennial year. The pageant was presented at the Harvard Loeb Drama Center and won the Bicentennial Grant for Boston, Cambridge, and surrounding areas. All ages from eight to sixty-five were invited to participate. Six schools were involved.

The author's first book, In Time for Tea and Other Childhood Stories, was published for family and friends. Her first book of poetry, Magic Is Where You Are, came out that same year and was dedicated to friends near and far, young and old. The poems gathered within this book span the years from 1946 to 1996.

Lee Pierce has been a teacher for many years and has used her collection of international dolls to teach and share cultures to both children and adults. She has traveled extensively through Latin America, Europe, and the United States.

Edwards Brothers Malloy
Oxnard, CA  USA
December 22, 2014